bullying

IS ANYONE LISTENING?

SHARP Literacy, Inc.
Student Historical Art Resource Program

This book was produced by SHARP Literacy, Inc. using the works submitted by the students involved in the Bullying Project.

This book is dedicated to you, and every child of the world. It is our hope that you know there are many people who care so much about your safety and want to help you.

We also dedicate this book to teachers, parents and guardians knowing that with open hearts and minds, working together, we can change so much.

Marlene M. Doerr, Executive Director SHARP Literacy, Inc.

SHARP Literacy, Inc.
Student Historical Art Resource Program

SHARP Literacy, Inc. is a non-profit 501(c)(3) educational organization.

Published by SHARP Literacy, Inc.
750 North Lincoln Memorial Drive Suite 311
Milwaukee, Wisconsin 53202-4018 USA
www.creativesharp.org

ISBN 0-9770816-4-8 Soft Cover
ISBN 0-9770816-5-6 Hard Cover

Printed in U.S.A

10 9 8 7 6 5 4 3 2 1

Acknowledgments

Ms. Sara Marquez, principal at Forest Home Avenue Elementary School, recognized the need for a student project that addressed the subject of bullying. Along with many other teachers, Ms. Marquez had witnessed numerous cases of bullying and was concerned about the lack of attention these incidents received from the community. She contacted SHARP Literacy, Inc. and asked if we would create a student project to address the issue of bullying. With the financial help of various donors and foundations, SHARP Literacy, Inc. took on this project through the successful *We Love to Learn* book program and *The Bullying Book Project* began to take shape. SHARP presented the opportunity to participate in the book project to teachers across the city. Teachers enthusiastically embraced the project and gave generously of their time and experience in helping SHARP formulate age-appropriate lessons, discussions, and assignments.

The Bullying Book Project set out to define the issue through the unique voices of SHARP students. Students were challenged to find words to describe their feelings as they wrote true accounts of situations they had experienced. In conducting their research for the written piece, students were encouraged to utilize the teachers and coaches at their schools. Students responded with a wide range of stories and poems on bullying and/or being confronted with violence. Once the research, reading, and writing were completed, students were then asked to illustrate their written composition for inclusion in the published book.

Over 500 students from seven Milwaukee-area schools participated in *The Bullying Book Project* to create *Bullying* Is Anyone Listening? As we work together to make schools a safer place, it is hoped that this book will be used as a guide for teachers, parents/guardians, students, and community partners to cease bullying behavior.

We also hope this book will accent the positive impact that people can have when we work together to solve social problems as they come to light.

— Marlene M. Doerr, Executive Director

A heartfelt thank you goes to the following funders who helped to make *Bullying* Is Anyone Listening? possible:

Elizabeth A. Brinn Foundation
Children's Hospital and Health System, Inc.
The Janus Foundation
Halbert and Alice Kadish Fund

This project has been a collaboration of:

Cardinal Stritch University
Children's Hospital and Health System, Inc.
Forest Home Avenue Elementary School
Greenfield Elementary School
Pat Lacocque
Marquette University Law Students
Milwaukee County Council, Boy Scouts of America
Poplar Creek Elementary School
St. Martini Lutheran School
Steffen Middle School
Urban Day 12th Street School
Urban Day 24th Street School

SHARP Literacy, Inc.
Student Historical Art Resource Program

A very special thank you to the SHARP Literacy, Inc. Board of Directors.

We are grateful to:

Francisco X. Mora for watercolor adaptations and contributions to the manuscript

Dan Saal for book design and layout

Special thanks to Andrew Doyle for creative thematic inspiration

Harry Russo, Marcela Garcia, Eladio Rivera—for Spanish translations

s Anyone Listening?

It was a sad experience to learn that all the children involved in this project had a common knowledge of bullying. Some more than others and at different times, but every single child had sensed the fear, pain, and embarrassment of being bullied.

Through their writing and pictures, some of the children retold their experiences in clear, simple, and precise form. For others, their responses were confusing, unclear, and erroneous. In most cases, they were already playing classic roles of the "Bully Syndrome" including: aggressor, victim, and bystander.

Some people believe that bullying is unavoidable because it happens all the time as a part of growing up. The truth is that bullying is an act of abuse that includes physical violence and emotional pain. Bullies, victims, and bystanders all need help.

It is often said that the most beautiful part of life is childhood. Childhood is only a short

Es una experiencia triste saber que todos los niños envueltos en este proyecto tienen un conocimiento común acerca del hostigamiento. Algunos participaron más que otros y en diferentes etapas, pero cada uno de los niños sintieron esa sensación, --ese dolor y esa situación vergonzosa de ser hostigado.

A través de sus trabajos escritos y dibujos, algunos de los niños recontaron sus experiencias en una forma clara, simple y precisa. Para otros, sus respuestas fueron de confusión, de incertidumbre y de pensamientos erróneos. En la mayoría de los casos, estuvieron expuestos a tomar diferentes papeles clásicos del "Síndrome de hostigamiento", tales como el del agresor, víctima y espectador.

Algunas personas piensan que el hostigamiento es inevitable ya que es parte del proceso de crecimiento. La verdad es que el hostigamiento es un acto de abuso que incluye

period of time where we fill our minds and hearts with everlasting memories of friendship, school days, warm summers, and winter holidays. In later years, thoughts of our childhood should bring joy and laughter. Yet for some, childhood memories are often tainted with painful, embarrassing, bitter, and upsetting incidents. It is a time they don't want to go back to because of the memory of being bullied.

The **look** of a bully, **loud** insulting words, the **smell** of fights, **taste** of fear, and **feeling** of pain should not be a part of a child's life. How deeply will such bad memories influence our children's lives?

We thank the children for opening their hearts to share their feelings and experiences. We thank the children for providing us with first hand accounts of being bullied and how their lives have been affected. In this book, the collection of stories, poems, and illustrations have been written and compiled by SHARP Literacy, Inc.

violencia física y dolor emocional. Los hostigadores, las víctimas y los espectadores siempre necesitan ayudan.
Con mucha frecuencia se dice que la parte más hermosa de la vida es la niñez. La infancia es solo un corto período de tiempo donde llenamos nuestras mentes y corazones con memorias eternas de amistad, de días escolares, de tibios veranos y de celebraciones de invierno. Años más tarde, pensamientos de nuestra infancia deben de traer diversión y risa. Pero para algunos, las memorias de la infancia son a veces teñidas con dolor, vergüenza, amargura y de incidentes infortunados. Esta época no la quieren recordar porque les trae recuerdos de hostigamiento.

La mirada de un hostigador, las palabras de insulto, el olor de peleas, el sabor del miedo y el sentimiento de dolor no deben formar parte de la vida de un niño. ¿Cómo estas malas memorias podrán influenciar la vida de nuestros niños? Agradecemos que nuestros niños hayan abierto sus corazones y compartido sus sentimientos y experiencias. Agradecemos a los niños por compartirnos sus relatos de hostigamiento y de cómo sus vidas han sido afectadas. En este libro, la colección de relatos poemas e ilustraciones han sido recopiladas por SHARP Literacy, Inc.

hear

see

smell

feel

Use All of Your Senses

Surprisingly most children are aware of the meaning of "Bullying."

Somehow everyone has been in the presence of a bully or under the shadow of someone who constantly practices this form of abuse.

Still there are a few that have no idea of the meaning or the consequences even though in many cases they are unknowing participants and already taken the roles of **Bully**, the **Victim** or the **Bystander**.

Here is where "bullying" is more dangerous and powerful because it can hide in the obscure corners of right and wrong.

Ask yourself these questions:

- What can I do if I **hear** that there is a bully in my school?
- What can I do if I **see** someone is being bullied?
- What can I do if I **smell** trouble coming directly at me?
- What can I do if I **feel** the pain caused by someone bullying me?
- What can I do if I **taste** the salt of my tears, or the warmth of my own blood?

Usa Todos Tus Sentidos

Sorprendentemente la mayoría de los niños están conscientes del significado de "hostigamiento".

De alguna manera todo el mundo ha estado en la presencia de un hostigador o bajo la sombra de alguien que constantemente práctica esta forma de abuso.

Aún hay algunos que no tienen idea alguna sobre del significado o de las consecuencias, aunque en muchos casos sin saberlo son participes y ya han adoptado el papel de hostigador, victima o del espectador.

Aquí es donde el "hostigamiento" es más peligroso y poderoso porque puede esconderse en los rincones oscuros del bien y del mal.

Hazte estas preguntas:

- ¿Qué puedo hacer si **he oído** que hay un hostigador en mi escuela?
- ¿Qué puedo hacer si **veo** a alguien que está siendo hostigado?
- ¿Qué puedo hacer si **huelo** un problema acercándose a mí?
- ¿Qué puedo hacer si **siento** el dolor causado por el hostigamiento de alguien?
- ¿Qué puedo hacer si **saboreo** la sal de mis lágrimas, o el calor de mi propia sangre?

taste

Enough

Everyday
I try to escape
the hallways
For I know
today
is the same as
Everyday.
I will not escape the torture,
I will not escape the pranks,
I will not escape the taunting.

Everyday
sprinting down the hallway
hiding
from "the bullies."

Everyday
the same pain
crying the same tears.
I wonder
When will I rise up
and
fend for myself?
When will I say
ENOUGH!
Perhaps
today.

Basta Ya

Todos los días
Trato de escapar
de los pasillos
Porque yo sé que
hoy
es lo mismo que
Todos los días.
No escaparé de las torturas,
No escaparé de las travesuras,
No escaparé de los insultos.

Todos los días
corro a toda velocidad por los pasillos
ocultándome
De "Los Hostigadores".

Todos los días
el mismo dolor,
llorando las mismas lagrimas.
Me pregunto
¿Cuándo podré levantarme
y
valerme por mí mismo?
Cuando podré decir
¡BASTA YA!
Tal vez
hoy.

I drew it because he's a little scary
and like a grizzly is scary too.

Yo lo dibuje porqué es un poco espantoso

Y como el oso gris es también espantoso .

Bus Bully

I think Bullies are not right, and I know how it feels to be bullied. I was in 2nd grade and I rode the bus. I sat with the same girl every day. There was a boy who sat by us. When he sat near us he would hit our hand and our heads and he would kick us. I felt hurt and sad; I would come home with cuts!

One day we hid. The next day we told the bus driver. He said, "I will take care of it." The bully had to sit in the front seat everyday and now I am not bullied anymore. Tell an adult about what is happening to you.

El Hostigador del Autobús

Yo pienso que no está bien ser hostigado por alguien y se como se siente uno cuando es hostigado. Estaba en segundo grado y abordé el autobús. Todos los días me sentaba en el mismo lugar en el autobús con la misma niña. Había un muchacho que siempre se sentaba cerca de nosotros. Cuando se sentaba cerca de nosotros, le gustaba pegarnos en las manos y en la cabeza y además nos pateaba. Yo me sentí lastimado y triste. ¡Yo llegaba a la casa con cortaduras!

Un día nos escondimos. Al siguiente día se lo dijimos al chofer. El nos dijo, "Resolveré eso". El hostigador tuvo que sentarse en el asiento del frente y ahora no soy hostigado. Dile a un adulto de lo que te está pasando.

Invisible

I am a second grader. I get bullied a lot from this boy. He has brown hair and is a lot taller than me. A couple of girls were mad at him, so they started to spread rumors about him. I guess he took it out on me.

Almost every day when I get to school, this boy flicks the top of my head. He makes sure there are no teachers around. Throughout the day, he calls me names like shrimp, small fry, and tiny.

Whenever he bullies me, he tells me if I tell anyone he'll be even meaner to me. So, I never tell an adult. At school, I feel invisible since none of the kids that hear him stand up for me. They just laugh. If I try to ignore him, he stomps on my foot until tears well up in my eyes.

What should I do?

Invisible

Estoy en segundo grado. Estoy siendo hostigado por este niño. Tiene el pelo castaño y es mucho más alto que yo. Un par de niñas se enojaron con él, y ellas comenzaron a decir rumores acerca de él. Supongo que él se desquitó conmigo.

Casi todos los días cuando llego a la escuela, este niño me golpea la cabeza. Él se asegura que no hayan maestros alrededor. Durante todo el día, él me llama apodos como camarón, pequeña papa frita y enano.

Cada vez que él me hostiga él me dice que si le digo a alguien él será aun más malo conmigo. Por lo tanto, yo nunca le digo a un adulto. En la escuela, me siento invisible, ya que ninguno de los niños que lo escuchan me defienden. Ellos simplemente se ríen. Si trato de ignorarlo, él me patea el pie hasta que los ojos se me llenan de lágrimas.

¿Qué debo hacer?

What should I do?

Help

One day out on the back playground, a boy walked up to me and said, "Give me your lunch or prepare for the beat down after school." So I handed him my money.

He repeated the same thing to me every day for the next two months. I was always hungry when I got home from school.

After a while, I decided it needed to stop. I was scared. I told my teacher. She did something I don't know how, but the boy stopped. I never saw that boy at our school again.

¡Socorro!

Un día en el patio trasero, un niño vino donde mi y me dijo, "Dame tu almuerzo o prepárate para los golpes después de la escuela". Así que le di mi dinero.

Durante los próximos dos meses todos los días me repitió la misma cosa. Siempre tenia hambre cuando llegaba a casa de la escuela.

Después de un tiempo, decidí que esto tenia que parar. Tenia miedo. Se lo conté a mi maestra. No se cómo, pero ella hizo algo y el nino paró. Nunca vi al niño otra vez en la escuela.

Guilt

Culpabilidad

When I bully people, I feel bad.

Cuando hostigo a personas, me siento mal.

I hurt others with my verbal and physical abuse.

Yo lastimo a otros con mi abuso verbal y físico.

When I bully, I feel really bad about myself.

Cuando hostigo, realmente me siento mal conmigo mismo.

I hate it when I talk bad about others.

Odio cuando me expreso mal de otros.

It just really gets on my last nerve.

Eso es justamente lo que me molesta.

But I don't like it when they talk about me.

Pero no me gusta cuando ellos se expresan mal de mi.

That is why I am always mad.

Es por eso que siempre estoy molesto.

This is why nobody likes me.

Es por eso que nadie me quiere.

I'm mean to other people.

Yo soy antipático con todas las personas.

They don't like my attitude.

A ellos no les gusta mi actitud.

When I bully someone, I feel bad.

Cuando hostigo a alguien, me siento mal.

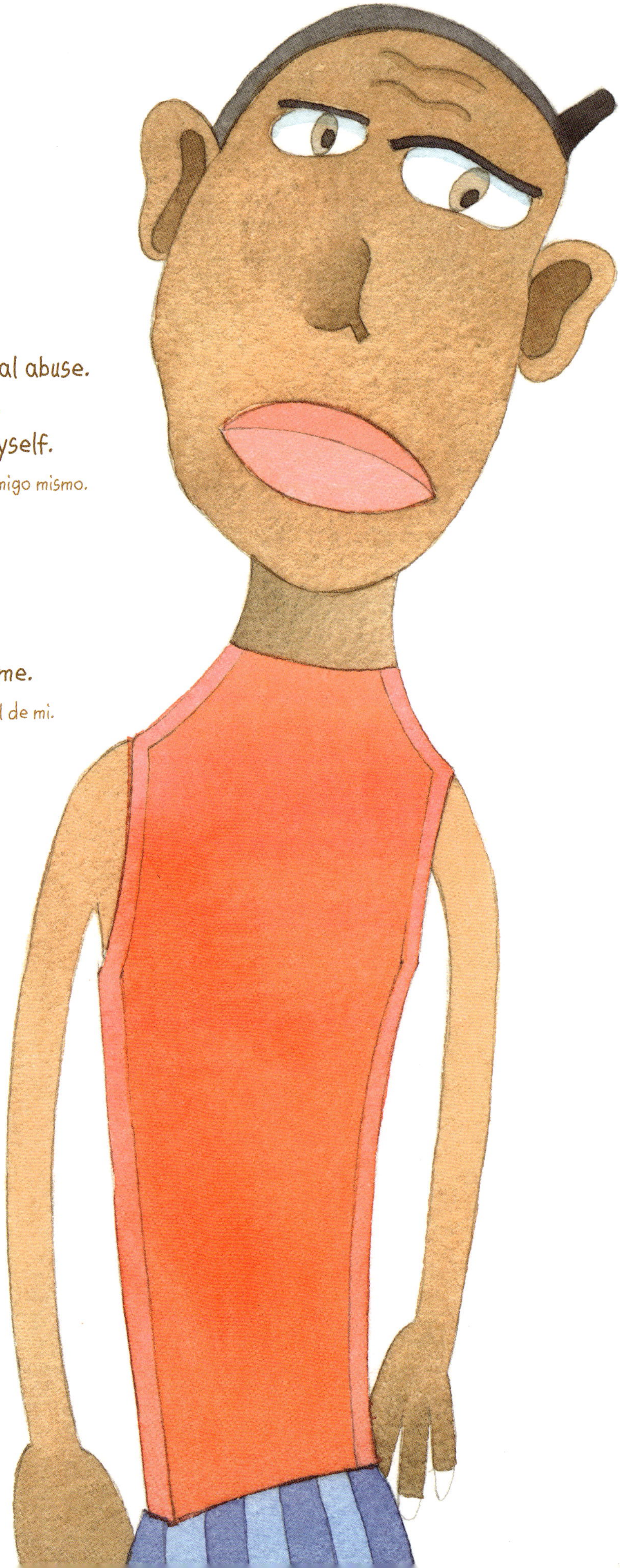

Abusive

Listen here.
Sit down and shut up.
I am your superior, I am your master.
I am better than you and always will be.
You are nothing to the world and nothing to me.
You are different, and I don't like your color.
I am going to shout out to the world.
I am going to shout out all your faults
And publicize your differences.

Abusivo

Escucha
Siéntate y calla.
Soy tu superior, soy tu maestro.
Yo soy mejor que tu y siempre seré.
Tú eres nada para el mundo y nada para mí.
Tú eres diferente, y no me gusta tu color.
Voy a gritar al mundo.
Voy a gritar todas tus fallas
Y dar a conocer tus diferencias.

I'm going to cause you pain, I'm going to make you hurt.
Because my life left nothing untouched, I express no emotion.
Because my life isn't the way I want, so yours can't be either.
Because I am unhappy, I am cruel and abusive to you.
Because I feel like it because I have nothing else to do.
I bully you because of what I lack in myself.

Voy a causarte dolor. Voy a hacerte daño.
Porque mi vida no deja nada intacto, no muestro emoción.
Porque mi vida no es de la manera que quiero, por lo tanto la tuya tampoco puede ser.
Porque soy infeliz, soy cruel y abusivo contigo.
Porque me da la gana y porque no tengo nada más que hacer.
Te hostigo por aquello que me falta en mi mismo.

What should I do if I hear that there is a bully in my school?

¿Qué puedo hacer si escucho que hay un hostigador en mi escuela?

Should I listen carefully?

¿Debo de estar escuchando más cuidadosamente?

What if my friends tell me that they are being bullied?

¿Qué tal si mis amigos me cuentan que los están hostigando?

Should I tell my teachers and my parents/guardians?

¿Debo decirles a mis maestros y a mis padres?

What are three solutions that would help solve the problem?

¿Cuáles son tres soluciones que pudieran ayudarme a resolver este problema?

Playground

I have been bullied about what I do and how I look. I have been bullied at school, at home, and on the playground.
I have been bullied in a lot of places, but I don't care.
I'm used to it now.

Patio de Recreo

He sido hostigado por lo que hago y por mi apariencia. He sido hostigado en la escuela, en mi casa y en el patio de recreo. He sido hostigado en muchos lugares, pero no me importa. Ya me he acostumbrado.

Homework

I got bullied by a boy at my old school. He made me do his homework. He cheated on his tests. He made me give him my soda. He would beat me up if I didn't give him something...anything.

Sometimes he pushed me. If I would put my hand up, he would punch my mouth; and, if that didn't work, he would really start to beat me up. When I got some money to buy books at the book sale, he would take my money too.

Tareas

Fui hostigado por un niño en mi otra escuela. Él me hizo hacer sus tareas. Hizo trampa en sus pruebas. Me hizo darle mi gaseosa. Me golpeaba si no le daba algo... cualquier cosa.

A veces me empujaba. Y si levantaba mi mano, él me golpeaba en mi boca, y si eso no funcionaba, él me comenzaba a golpear de verdad. Cuando llegaba con un poco de dinero para comprar libros en la venta de libros, me quitaba el dinero también.

he would punch my mouth

The Short Kid and the Giant

"Hey fatso," yelled the short kid to the giant on the playground. All of the kids crowded around the giant, like vultures crowding around a doomed beast. He was new in school, you see, and no one knew how he would react to the thug in town. The person you didn't mess with if you wanted to stay alive, or the person who could crush your image in a flash. The person you didn't want to meet in the wrong place. The gentle giant turned away and walked back into school, but before he could escape inside the short kid yelled again, "Hey fatso, why ya running, you afraid of me?" The gentle giant just walked away into the school with no reaction to the insult.

The short student was very persistent. He never failed to insult the gentle giant of a boy but was always disappointed at his calm reaction. The bully, like all bullies, thought that no one would ever come to the rescue of his victim. These insults, however, began to anger the other students who had been observing these incidents. A few weeks later things came to a head.

The short kid did his stuff. This time instead of walking away, the gentle giant looked down at the short kid and said, "How is the weather down there shorty?" Another kid chipped in saying, "Hey punk, why don't you take your useless junk with you and get outta here?" While this statement was a little long winded, it had the desired effect.

El Niño Pequeño y el Gigante

"Oye Gordo". Gritó el pequeño niño al gigante en el patio de recreo. Todos los niños rodearon al gigante, como buitres alrededor de una bestia entorpecida. Era nuevo en la escuela, tú ves, nadie sabia como iba a reaccionar ante el bravucón del pueblo. La persona con el cual no debías meterte si querías permanecer vivo en la escuela, o la persona que podía destruir tu imagen en segundos. La persona con el cual no te quisieras encontrar en el lugar equivocado. El tierno gigante se marchó y regresó a la escuela, pero antes de que se pudiera escapar ahí estaba el niño pequeño gritando una vez más, "Oye gordo, ¿por qué huyes, me tienes miedo? El tierno gigante se regresó a la escuela sin ninguna reacción al insulto.

El niño pequeño fue muy insistente. No paró de insultar al tierno gigante pero siempre estuvo disgustado por su calmada reacción. El hostigador, como todos los hostigadores, pensaba que nadie nunca vendría a rescatar a su victimas. Estos insultos, sin embargo, comenzaron a enojar a los otros estudiantes que habían estado observando estos incidentes. Semanas más tarde los cosas cambiaron.

El niño pequeño hizo de las suyas. En esta ocasión en vez de alejarse, el tierno gigante miró al niño pequeño y le dijo, "¿Cómo está el clima allá abajo?" Otro niño saltó y dijo, "Oye basura, ¿porqué no recoges tu basura y te largas de aquí?" A pesar que esta declaración tomó un poco de tiempo, logró el efecto deseado. Molesto por estos comentarios detestables, el niño pequeño trató de tirarse sobre el tierno gigante. Desgraciadamente, falló y calló enfrente del director, quien había visto todo. Cuando el niño pequeño salió de la oficina del director, el tierno gigante y sus amigos lo estaban esperando. El pequeño esperaba recibir una dosis de su propia medicina y se preparó para lo peor. El tierno gigante, sin embargo, le extendió su mano de amistad. La mano que lo pudo haber destruido. La mano que pudo haber comenzado una batalla. La mano que calmó todo. Un conflicto que pudo haber durado por años fue detenido por una simple frase pronunciada en un segundo, "Seamos amigos."

Infuriated by these obnoxious remarks, the short kid tried to jump on top of the gentle giant. Unfortunately, he missed and landed right in front of the principal, who had been watching the whole thing. When the short kid came out of the principal's office, the gentle giant and his friends were waiting for him. The short kid expected to get a dose of his own medicine and braced himself for the worst. The gentle boy, however, simply held out his hand in friendship. The hand that could have destroyed. The hand that could have started battle. The hand that settled everything. A conflict that could have lasted for years was stopped by a single phrase uttered in a second, "Let's be friends."

Tell someone

If you hear a bully talking, tell an adult or a friend. When I was in 3rd grade I had a bully pushing me and talking to me, and it made me feel bad all the time. He said terrible things about me that were not true. I was getting angry with myself.

I couldn't take it anymore so I talked with my mom and dad about it. They told me that I had to forget it so I tried not to think about it for a while. I listened to them, but I couldn't forget it for long. I told them I couldn't forget it because he was always there treating me like I was no one.

My parents said that everyday I had to come home and talk to them about my day and that helped me to figure out what to do and how to handle my problems. So if you have a bully hurting you talk to an adult or to a good friend.

Dile a Alguien

Si escuchas a un hostigador hablando, dile a un adulto o a un amigo. Cuando yo estaba en 3er grado, un hostigador me empujaba y me hablaba y me hacia sentir mal todo el tiempo. El decía cosas horribles de mi que no eran verdad. Me estaba enojando conmigo mismo.

No pude soportarlo más, y hablé con mamá y papá de eso. Ellos me dijeron que yo tenia que olvidarme de eso por un tiempo. Yo los escuché, pero no pude dejar de pensar en él por mucho tiempo. Yo les dije que no podía olvidarlo porque él siempre estaba tratándome como si yo fuera nadie.

Mis padres me dijeron que todos los días tenia que llegar a la casa y hablar con ellos de mi día. Eso me ayudó a planear que hacer y cómo manejar mis problemas. Así que si hay un hostigador que te está heriendo, habla con adulto o con un buen amigo.

like I was no one

Name Calling

Poniendo Sobrenombres

I've always been treated badly.
Siempre me han tratado mal.
Bullies call me names like "UGLY."
Me hostigan diciéndome nombres como "feo".
I always feel left out,
Siempre me siento solo.
When no one lets me play.
Cuando no me permiten jugar con ellos,
I always feel lonely,
Siempre me siento solo,
When no one wants to play with me.
Cuando nadie quiere jugar conmigo,
Some bullies yell at me,
Algunos hostigadores me gritan,
So I run away.
y por eso me voy corriendo,
I don't want to see bullies again.
No quiero ver un hostigador otra vez.

Hurtful

Fat
Fatty
Hog
Hippopotamus
Fat boy
Toothpick
Crybaby
Butthead
Freak
Loser
Freckle face
Nose picker
Gay
Stupid
Dumb
Shorty

Hiriente

Gordo
Gordito
Cerdo
Hipopótamo
Niño gordo
Palillo de diente
Llorón
Cabezón
Anormal
Perdedor
Cara de pecas
Saca moco
Homosexual
Estúpido
Tonto
Enano

calling him names

Silence

My story is about a boy who is always bullied. This girl bullies him and he doesn't say anything. The girl is always punching him. More than one person is bullying this person. They think they can take advantage of him because he doesn't say anything. No matter what, he will not tell the teachers.

I always see the person punching him or calling him names. Sometimes I feel like saying something, but I don't.

Silencio

Mi historia es acerca de un niño que es siempre hostigado. Esa niña lo hostiga y él no dice nada. La niña siempre lo está golpeando. Más de una persona lo hostiga. Ellos piensan que pueden sacar provecho de él porque no dice nada. No importa lo que pase, él no le diría nada a los maestros.

Siempre veo a esta persona golpeándolo o poniéndole sobrenombres. Algunas veces siento decir algo, pero no lo hago.

What should I do if I see someone that is being bullied?

¿Qué debo hacer si veo a alguien que está siendo hostigado?

Should I just watch and do nothing?

¿Debo vigilar y no hacer nada?

Should I run as fast as I can or should I close my eyes?

¿Debo de huir tan rápido como pueda o debo de cerrar mis ojos?

Should I tell my teachers and my parents/guardians?

¿Debo decirles a mis maestros y a mis padres?

What are three solutions that would help solve the problem?

¿Cuáles son tres soluciones que pudieran ayudarme a resolver este problema?

I don't do anything about it

Coward

Everyday I see this kid get picked on. I don't like him very much, and he doesn't like me. He's kind of weird and doesn't fit in at all. Nobody likes him and nobody wants to be his friend.

Everyday I see him get knocked around and I hate it. I'm such a coward because I don't do anything about it. I cringe whenever I see him get picked on, and I want to do something. I know it is dumb that I don't stick up for him because I would get called a name, but being called a name is also bullying, and I don't like it.

There is another kid who does stick up for him. I wish I could be brave like that. I guess I am kind of a bully for not sticking up for him or trying to stop the bullying. It is bad and I wish it would stop, but the world isn't like that. Maybe I will stick up for him, and I know it would feel good.

Cobarde

Todos los días, veo a este niño que lo fastidian. El no me cae muy bien, y yo tampoco le caigo muy bien a él. Él es un poco extraño y no encaja con nadie. A nadie le gusta él y nadie quiere ser su amigo.

Todos los días veo como lo fastidian y lo odio. Soy un cobarde porque no hago nada al respecto. Me encojo cuando veo que lo fastidian, y quiero hacer algo. Sé que es tonto que no doy la cara por él o que no trato de detener el hostigamiento, porque no quiero que me llamen sobrenombres, porque el ser llamado sobrenombre es también acoso, y no me gusta.

Hay otro niño que si lo defiende. Me gustaría ser así de valiente. Supongo que soy como un hostigador porque no lo defiendo o trato de parar el hostigamiento. Esta mal y deseo que pare, pero el mundo no es así. Quizás lo defienda, y se que se sentirá bien.

NY
10

I don't like it

Explode

Estallar

When they pick on me
Cuando ellos me señalan para molestarme,
it's annoying.
me encuentro incomodo.
I don't like it!
¡No me gusta!
I feel very angry when they pick on me.
Me siento muy molesto cuando me molestan.
I try to ignore them,
Trato de ignorarlos,
but they are telling me in my ear.
pero ellos me están hablando en mi oído.
When they talk I know it isn't true.
Cuando ellos hablan, yo se que no es verdad.
I feel my head hurting
Me siento con la cabeza adolorida
from what they are saying.
de que ellos estén hablando.
My head feels like
Mi cabeza se siente
it is going to explode.
como si fuera a explotar

Cyberbully

A bullying situation is when people treat you bad and tell you things that aren't supposed to be said.

A cyberbully is a person who writes things on the Internet and texting and they call you bad things on the phone.

I was bullied by a person. I was a victim. A bully makes me scared. Sometimes, they make you pay. I promise not to be a bully. I would never be a bystander either.

Hostigador Cibernético

Un situación de hostigamiento es cuando la gente te trata mal y te dicen cosas que se supone que no deben de ser dichas.

Un hostigador cibernético es una persona que ya sea escribe cosas en el Internet o por mensaje de texto o te dice cosas malas por el teléfono.

Yo fui hostigado por una persona. Yo fui una victima. Un hostigador me asusta. Algunas veces ellos te hacen que tú les pagues. Prometo no ser un hostigador. Yo nunca sería un espectador tampoco.

Bitterness

I observe you in all your victory.
Enjoying, flaunting and basking in the fullness of your character.
You are adored by all.
Their taunts do not plague you.
I'm sure you have strength and beauty as well.

Amargura

Te observo en toda tu victoria.
Disfrutando, presumiendo y envuelto en la plenitud de tu carácter.
Eres adorado por todos.
Sus burlas no te atormentan.
Estoy seguro de que tienes la fortaleza y la belleza también.

But your strength is no barrier or obstacle for me.
The look on your face when my words reach your eyes
Strikes a feeling that I can place.
My power over you seems unending.

Pero tu fortaleza no es una barrera u obstáculo para mí.
La mirada en tu cara cuando mis palabras llegan a tus ojos
causa un sentimiento que puedo identificar.
Mi poder sobre ti parece eterno.

I can remember that look staring me back in the mirror.
Those days long ago when another towered over me.
When another destroyed me bit by bit,
Voicing all my apparent flaws. They made me feel unworthy.

Puedo recordar aquella mirada fijándose en mi en el espejo.
Aquellos días cuando hace mucho tiempo atrás otro se amontonaba sobre mí.
Cuando otro me destruía poco a poco,
expresando todos mis defectos obvios. Ellos me hicieron sentir indigno.

Is my revenge justified? I now pay the price of guilt.
I see the continuous bitterness of the circle.

¿Es mi venganza justificada? Ahora pago el precio de la culpa.
Veo la amargura continua del círculo.

destroy me bit by bit

Anxiety

When bullying occurs, I am usually the bystander of it. I am the person who watches the event happen. I have watched the bully push books out of the person's hands. I have watched the bully trip the person in the hallways. I have watched the bully call the helpless people names. I admit that I was one of those laughing bystanders who didn't do anything but stand there.

Thinking back on all of those times when I just stood there and watched the event take place, makes my stomach do summersaults over and over and over. It felt like a giant had punched me in the stomach.

Bullying in my opinion is terrifying for kids. It happens all the time. I feel bad for all the people I've seen that have been picked on. I regret not having done something about it. Bullying can be like robbing a bank because you rob the victims of their happiness in life.

Ansiedad

Cuando el hostigamiento ocurre, por lo general soy un espectador. Soy la persona que veo el evento ocurrir. He visto al hostigador tirar los libros de sus manos. He visto al hostigador ponerle el pie en los pasillos. He visto al hostigador llamarle sobrenombre a los indefensos. Admito que fui uno de los espectadores que me reí, que no hice nada sino solo quedarme ahí parado.

Cuando pienso en esos momentos cuando solo miré lo ocurrido, hace que mi estomago de vueltas una y otra vez. Siento como que un gigante me golpeó en el estomago.

En mi opinión el hostigamiento es aterrorizador para los niños. Ocurre todo el tiempo. Me siento mal por todas las personas que han sido victimas. Me arrepiento de no haber hecho nada al respecto. El hostigamiento es como robar un banco porque robas a las victimas su felicidad en la vida.

Tornado

Whenever a bully passes by, it's like a path of
destruction a tornado leaves behind.

Tornado

Cada vez que pasa un hostigador, es como un camino de
destrucción que un tornado deja atrás.

The debris left are bruises and scars.
Some might join, others may watch.
Few try to stop it, and at times, it grows and grows.

Los escombros son moretones y cicatrices.
Algunos se pueden unir, otros nada mas observan.
Pocos tratan de detenerlo, y, en ocasiones, crece y crece.

The hallways can be pathways of destruction and shame,
for a bully has just passed by.

Los pasillos pueden ser caminos de destrucción y vergüenza,
porque un hostigador acaba de pasar.

Help me weather the storm.

Ayúdame a pasar la tormenta.

Harassment

Hostigamiento

I've watched bullying before.

He visto hostigamiento anteriormente.

Let me tell you, it's not fun.

Déjame decirte, eso no es divertido.

First they either call you names or hit you hard.

Primero te dicen nombres o te golpean fuerte.

Then when they're done hitting you,

Cuando terminan de golpearte,

they make fun of you because you are hurt.

Ellos hacen burla de ti, porque estas herido.

Then they walk away to do it to someone else.

Entonces se van caminando para hacerselo a alguna otra persona.

What should I do if I smell the blood from a fight?

¿Qué puedo hacer si huelo el polvo de una pelea?

What should I do if someone is being pushed down into the dirt?

¿Qué debo hacer si alguien está empujando a alguien al suelo?

What are things I can do to make them not smell fear?

¿Cuáles son las cosas que debo hacer para que no huelan el miedo?

Should I tell my teachers and my parents/guardians?

¿Debo decirles a mis maestros y a mis padres?

What are three solutions that would help solve the problem?

¿Cuáles son tres soluciones que pudieran ayudarme a resolver este problema?

Save Me

Salvame

I am depressed in your presence.
Estoy deprimido en tu presencia.
My mind retreats into a trap when I see the
Mi mente se retrocede hacia una trampa cuando veo los
Bruises and bumps.
moretones y los golpes.
Faceless people watch from behind.
Personas sin rostros miran de lejos.
No emotions or sympathy in their faces.
No hay emociones o simpatía en sus rostros.
I cry for help but only deaf ears listen.
Pido ayuda, pero sólo oídos ensordecidos escuchan.
I lift my hand from the dirty ground.
Levanto mi mano del terreno sucio.
I reach high for a lift and someone to hold.
Trato de alcanzar algo que me levante y alguien quien me agarre.
I watch it fall to the endless pit.
Veo como cae al abismo.
No one takes time to notice, why would they?
Nadie se toma el tiempo para verme, ¿por qué lo habrán de hacer?
"It's not me" they say.
"No soy yo" ellos dicen
"It's not my problem."
"No es mi problema."
"Someone else will do it."
"Alguien más lo hará."
I will just wait for my savior to come.
Solo esperaré a que llegue mi Salvador.

Encolerizado

Cuando soy hostigado, realmente me siento enojado. Ellos hablan de mí. Ellos hablan acerca de mi mamá y de los miembros de mi familia. Ellos me pegan, me avientan y me empujan. Cuando tengo dinero ellos dicen que soy su mejor amigo. Yo me siento mal porque yo se que eso no es verdad. Algunas veces quiero que la persona me está hostigando no venga a la escuela.

Irate

When I get bullied, I feel really mad. They talk about me. They talk about my mom and family members. They hit, push, and shove me. When I have money, they say I am their best friend. I get mad because I know it is not true. Sometimes I want the person who's bullying me not to come to school.

Fear

They were always calling me names. They were teasing me because I was small. They always hit me. I never told the teacher or my parents because I was scared they were going to beat me up.

Temor

Siempre me estaban llamando con sobrenombres. Ellos hacían bromas porque yo era pequeño. Siempre me pegaban. Nunca dije nada a la maestra o a mis padres porque tenia miedo de que ellos me fueran a pegar.

Cruel

I have been bullied since I was in third grade. I went to my bus stop. When I got on, everybody on the bus started calling me Jelly Sandwich! That name is so dumb. Who calls a person a jelly sandwich?

Crueldar

He sido hostigado desde el tercer grado. Fui a mi parada del autobús. Cuando subí el autobús, todos comenzaron a llamarme "¡Sándwich de Mermelada!" Ese nombre tan ridículo ¿Quién llamaría a una persona "Sándwich de Mermelada"?

He sido hostigado por lo que hago, por lo que me interesa y por mi apariencia. He sido hostigado en la escuela, en la casa y en el patio de recreo. He sido hostigado en muchos lugares, pero no me importa. Ya estoy acostumbrado.

I have been bullied because of what I do and care about and how I look. I have been bullied at school, at home, and on the playground. I have been bullied in a lot of places, but I don't care. I'm used to it now.

Stares

I am from her hateful glares
From "did you hear about her," as everyone stares
The gossip, the rumors, and the made up lies
From the writing on the wall that made me cry.

Miradas

Soy parte de su mirada de odio.
De "Oíste eso acerca de ella" al mismo tiempo que todos miran
El chisme, los rumores y las mentiras inventadas
Desde las palabras escritas en la pared que me hacen llorar.

I am from being scared to come to school
And from worrying about what she's going to do
I am from feeling useless and thrown away
This feeling I carry with me every day.

Desde venir con miedo a la escuela
Y de preocuparme acerca de lo que ella va a hacer
Desde sentirme inútil y desechado
Este es el sentimiento que yo llevo conmigo todos los días.

I am from the final straw
Confronting her as others stare at me with awe
It's done, it's over. I can't deal anymore.
It's time for me to be strong.

Desde la última gota
Confrontándola mientras otros me miran con asombro
Está hecho, está terminado, No puedo más con esto
Es el momento para yo ser fuerte.

Coerced

I saw someone get bullied. It happened in the back of the school. The bully had a ripped coat and hat. The bully wanted the kid's lunch money.

The kid would not give it up. The bully got mad and hit the kid very hard.

Then the bully said, "I'll give you one more chance to give it up!" The kid still wouldn't give it up. This time the bully hit him harder. The bully got real mad and screamed, "Now!"

The kid only gave him a dollar. One kid came and tried to help him, but he just got hit too. The bully said, "Give it all if you know what's good for you."

The kid finally gave the bully his money. We watched the bully buy food. He looked hungry and poor. Maybe that's why he is a bully.

Obligado

Vi a alguien siendo acosado. Sucedió en la parte trasera de la escuela. El hostigador tenía un abrigo roto y un sombrero. El hostigador quería el dinero del almuerzo del niño.

El niño no se lo quería dar. El hostigador se enfadó y golpeó al niño muy duro.

Entonces, el hostigador dijo: "Te daré una oportunidad más para que me lo des!" El niño todavía no se lo daba. Esta vez el hostigador le golpeó con más fuerza. El hostigador se enojó más aun y gritó, "¡Ahora!"

El niño sólo le dio un dólar. Un niño vino y trató de ayudarlo, pero también fue golpeado. El hostigador dijo: "Dámelo si sabes lo que te conviene."

El niño finalmente le dio el dinero al hostigador. Vimos al hostigador comprar alimentos. Parecía hambriento y pobre. Tal vez por eso él es un hostigador.

Loneliness

Soledad

I go to school. I always have to walk. The bullies will chase me.

Voy a la escuela. Siempre tengo que caminar. Los hostigadores siempre me persiguen.

They will hit me until I hurt.

Ellos me golpearán hasta lastimarme.

At recess, I will go to a lonely place.

En el recreo, yo iré a un lugar solitario.

I will feel like I do not even live on earth.

Me sentiré como si no viviera en la Tierra.

Then I go to the bullies. I tell them to stop, but they start to laugh.

Luego voy para donde están los hostigadores. Les digo que paren, pero ellos comienzan a reírse.

When I get home, I feel so happy that this is over.

Cuando llego a casa, me siento feliz de que esto haya terminado.

How have I felt when I was being bullied?

¿Cómo me sentí cuando fui hostigado?

What should I do to help someone who has felt the pain of daily abuse?

¿Qué debo hacer para ayudar a alguien que diariamente siente el abuso?

What should I do to show I care?

¿Qué debo hacer para mostrarle respeto a otros?

Should I tell my teachers and my parents/guardians?

¿Debo decirles a mis maestros y a mis padres?

What are three solutions that would help solve the problem?

¿Cuáles son tres soluciones que pudieran ayudarme a resolver este problema?

Bystanders

Espectadores

She is walking into school,
Ella va camino a la escuela.
Hiding behind her long hair and her stack of books.
Escondida detrás de su pelo largo y su pila de libros.
She looks for them, the girls that make her life a living hell.
Ella las busca, las niñas que le hacen su vida un infierno.
She looks left and then right.
Mira hacía la izquierda y luego hacía derecha.
A sigh of relief, they are no where to be found.
Un suspiro de alivio, ellas no se encuentran por ninguna parte.
Then a push in the back as she slowly turns.
Un empujón en la espalda mientras ella se da vuelta lentamente.
There they stand, glaring, laughing.
Ahí están, deslumbrantes, riéndose.
One pushes her books to the ground.
Una de ellas tira sus libros al suelo.
Another calls her "ugly," the others just stand and watch.
Otra la llama "fea", las otras solo observan.
The nearby jock points and laughs.
Aquellos a su alrededor la señalan y se ríen.
No one stops to help her, no one intervenes.
Nadie se detiene a ayudarla, nadie interviene,
She cries and runs and runs far away.
Ella grita y corre y corre lejos.
She wants just to fly away.
Ella sólo quiere volar.
Never to see taunting eyes again.
Nunca ver esos ojos burlones otra vez.
For everyday it's the same pain.
Porque todos los días es el mismo dolor.
Some days are worse than others.
Algunos días son peores que otros.
She leaves and goes to a place where she will not return.
Ella se aleja y se va a un lugar del cual no regresará.
She is not at school the next day or any day after.
Ella no está en la escuela el siguiente día, o cualquier día después.
She is gone to a sanctuary of her own.
Ella se ha ido a su propio santuario.
She is gone forever.
Ella se ha ido para siempre.

Angry

I was walking in the hallway going to the bathroom. When I got to the bathroom, someone was behind me, and I was pushed. "Next time get out of my way," he said. So I got up and went into a stall. I tried to wait for awhile. When I came out, he was still in the bathroom. I started washing my hands, and he pushed me again. He said I was using his sink. Then he said, "If you tell the teacher, I will beat you up until you are in the hospital." So I walked away.

At the end of the day, I was going to get my little brother. He came and pushed me again. Again I just walked away. When my brother and I were walking away, he was calling me names. I was glad that we could leave with my mom. I want to hurt him, but I did nothing! I feel very mad!!!

Enojado

Estaba caminando por el pasillo hacia el baño. Cuando llegue al baño, alguien estaba detrás de mi y fui empujado. "La próxima vez salte de mi camino," él dijo. Me levanté y entré a un compartimiento en el baño. Trate de esperar a que pasará el tiempo. Cuando salí, él aún estaba en el baño. Yo comencé a lavarme las manos y él empezó a empujarme otra vez. Dijo que yo estaba usando su lavamanos. Entonces él dijo, "Si se lo dices al maestro, te voy a pegar hasta que estés en el hospital". Me fui caminando de allí.

Al final del día, iba a ir a buscar a mi hermanito. El vino y me empujó otra vez. Me alejé de él otra vez. Mientras mi hermanito y yo nos alejábamos, él comenzó a llamarnos nombres. Estuve satisfecho que pudimos irnos con mi mamá. Yo quise herirlo, pero no hice nada. ¡Me siento muy enojado!

Panic

I was playing with my brothers when these two older kids came. They said that there was candy in the garbage can. I was only 4, and I didn't know any better, so I went to look inside. There wasn't any candy, I was confused. Then before I could say stop, they put me inside of the garbage can. I was stuck in that big, deep and dark garbage can with my brothers. We were all crying very loud and feeling panicked until my Grandma came to help us get out. I will never forget those two older kids that bullied us that day.

Pánico

Yo estaba jugando con mis hermanos cuando dos niños mayores vinieron. Dijeron que había dulces en el bote de la basura. Tenia solamente 4 años. No entendía bien las cosas. Y decidí buscar el dulce en el bote de basura. No había ningún dulce, estaba confundido. Antes de poder decirles que me dejaran quieto, me hecharon dentro del bote. Estaba atrapado en ese grande, profundo y oscuro bote con mis hermanos. Estábamos llorando muy fuerte y sintiendo pánico hasta que mi abuela vino a ayudarnos a salir de allí. Nunca olvidaré a esos dos niños mayores que nos hostigaron ese día

Taste Fear

Being bullied is horrible. It feels terrible when they call you names or people threaten you. I taste fear; you feel afraid and never want to go back to school because you want to feel safe and protected. I feel sick to my stomach. Bullies don't know that they might be hurting you from the inside.

It hurts deep in you. I haven't been bullied like some of my friends have, but I do know how it feels to be called ugly names and punched when no one is noticing.

Probando el Temor

Es horrible ser hostigado. Se siente terrible cuando te llaman con sobrenombres o cuando te amenazan. Al probar temor, te sientes asustado y no quieres regresar a la escuela porque quieres sentirte seguro y protegido. Me siento enfermo del estomago. Los hostigadores no saben que te están hiriendo desde adentro.

Esto te duele profundamente. No he sido hostigado como lo han sido algunos de mis amigos, pero si se como se siente cuando te llaman nombres feos y te golpean cuando nadie está mirando.

Imperfections

There are bad people that make fun of our flaws and how we are. When someone is teasing me I feel bad, angry, upset and at the same time stressed.

All human nature has failings, but some people think that they don't have any. They shouldn't tease because they have defects too. When other kids tease me I feel scared and angry. I feel like hitting them.

People shouldn't judge other people that are different or have defects. We all have feelings; and although I don't understand the bully's attitude, I'm sure that sooner or later they will have to pay for the damage that they have caused other people.

What goes around comes around in the circle of life.

Imperfecciones

Hay personas malas que se burlan que de nuestros defectos y de cómo somos. Cuando alguien se está burlando de mí me siento mal, enojado y a la misma vez estresado.

Todos los seres humanos tenemos fallas, aunque algunos piensan que no tienen ninguna. No deberían burlarse porque ellos también tienen defectos. Cuando otros niños se burlan de mí me siento con miedo y enojado. Me dan deseos de pegarle.

Las personas no deberían juzgar a otras personas que son diferentes o que tienen defectos. Todos tenemos sentimientos, y aunque no entiendo la actitud del hostigador, estoy seguro de que tarde o temprano tendrán que pagar por el daño que han causado a otras personas.

En el círculo de la vida aquello que da vuelta se regresa.

feel bad

Bullies are mean people. Did

U know they just do it because they want to

Look tough. Others do it because they need

Love from their parents or friends.
But sometimes they need help from people like

You.

Adiós

Una broma sin sentido sale de sus labios,
El último nervio de su pesadilla se desgarra.
Un duro golpe al lado de su mejilla,
Debajo, sus pies se debilitan.
Se siente ridiculizada.
Ella no puede soportar sentirse constantemente como una tonta.
Rostro sangriento, palma de la mano sudorosa, respiración profunda.
Ella se arrastra a su casa debido a la golpiza.

Ella hace contacto visual con el terreno.
Si sólo hubiera alguien alrededor.
Demasiada vergüenza para mantener su cabeza en alto.
El dolor dentro de ella se acumula rápidamente.
Ella deambula a su casa y entra por la puerta.
Mira a su familia, ya no lo puede soportar más.

Ella se deja caer sobre su cama.
Suavemente descansando su cabeza golpeada.
Ella le deja saber a sus seres queridos el porqué.
Mientras escribe en una carta su último adiós.
El fin estaba ahí, lo podía sentir correr por su cuerpo.

Goodbye

A senseless joke runs from her lips,
The last nerve of her nightmare rips.
A heavy blow to the side of her cheek,
Underneath, her feet get weak.
She feels the spotlight of ridicule.
She can't bear constantly looking like a fool.
Bloody face, sweaty palms, deep breathing.
She drags herself home from the beating.

She makes eye contact with the ground.
If only there was someone around.
Too much shame to pick her head up.
The pain inside her quickly builds up.
She wanders home and walks through the door.
Looking at her family, she can't take it any more.

She collapses on her bed.
Gently resting her bruised head.
She lets her dearest ones know why.
As she inscribes in a letter her last goodbye.
The end was there, she could feel it run through her.

What should I do if I taste the salt of my own tears?

¿Qué debo hacer si saboreo la sal de mis propias lagrimas?

Should I stay and do nothing?

¿Debo quedarme sin hacer nada?

Should I run away and tell no one?

¿Debo correr tan rápido como pueda y buscar ayuda?

Should I tell my teachers and my parents/guardians?

¿Debo decirles a mis maestros y a mis padres?

What are three solutions that would help solve the problem?

¿Cuáles son tres soluciones que pudieran ayudarme a resolver este problema?

Assistant Principal's Story

This is a story related to us from an Assistant Principal of a local public school. The Assistant Principal was given an anonymous note that a second grade child was being manipulated and bullied by an older child.

The young bullied child was told to go home and bring back a dollar to the bully. If the bullied child did not bring the dollar to school, she was told by the bully that he would "Beat her up." For the bullied child, this meant she would suffer physical pain or she and her family would be harassed by the bully and others. Out of concern for her family and herself, the bullied child brought a dollar to school each day. It was only after a month of bringing a dollar to school that the situation came to the attention of the school's Assistant Principal.

Un Relato del Subdirector

Esto es una historia que un subdirector de una escuela pública local nos redacto. El subdirector recibió una nota anónima que decía que había un niño mayor que estaba manipulando y hostigando a una estudiante del segundo grado.

El hostigador le dijo a la niña hostigada que vaya a su casa y le trajera un dólar. Si la niña no traía el dólar a la escuela, el hostigador le iba a dar una golpiza. Esto significaba que la niña hostigada iba a sufrir un dolor físico o que ella y su familia iban a ser hostigados por el hostigador y otros. Debido a su preocupación por su familia y por si misma, la niña hostigada trajo un dólar a la escuela todos los días para que no le dieran. Luego de haber pasado un mes trayendo un dólar a la escuela, el subdirector se entero de la situación.

¿Qué representa para un niño pobre traer un dólar a la escuela todos los días? Puede que el niño no tenga dinero para su almuerzo, puede que tenga que robarle a sus compañeros, familia y/o amigos debido al miedo sobre lo que pueda pasar. Puede que tenga que buscar en los botes de basura algo que pueda vender. Definitivamente quiere decir que el niño no puede concentrarse en los asuntos escolares, sino en cómo y de dónde puede conseguir el dinero diariamente para el hostigador.

What does it mean for a child of poverty to bring a dollar to school each day? It may mean that child does not have lunch money; it may mean stealing from peers, family and/ or friends because of fear of what may happen. It may mean going through trash dumpsters in alleys looking for something to sell. It definitely means that child does not concentrate on school matters, but on how and where to find money for the bully each day.

After much conversation with the bullied child, it was noticed that there were small pinch marks on the little second grader's arms. These cruel marks where a reminder to her to bring a dollar back to school each day or something much worse was being planned.

Después de muchas conversaciones con la niña hostigada, el subdirector se fijo en unas marcas pequeñas en los brazos de la niña de segundo grado. Eran pellizcos. Estas marcas crueles eran un recordatorio de que ella tenia que traer un dólar a la escuela todos los días o que algo mucho peor le iba a suceder.

Cuando fue a la oficina del subdirector, el hostigador negó haber molestado a la niña o de haber estado envuelto, pero muchos compañeros de la niña hostigada vieron lo que había sucedido. A pesar de que estos niños no habían dicho o hecho nada anteriormente, en la presencia del subdirector, ellos estaban dispuestos a decir la verdad y dijeron—"Si, todo esto ocurrió." Cuando el padre del hostigador recibió la llamada sobre el comportamiento de su hijo, el padre contestó "Envíenlo a la casa. Yo le daré una buena paliza."

When called into the Assistant Principal's office, the bully denied any wrong doing or involvement, but many peers of the bullied child saw what had happened. Although the children did not say or do anything at the time of the incident, in the presence of the Assistant Principal, they were willing to stand up for the bullied child and say, "Yes, this all did take place." When the bully's parent was called about the bullying, the parent's reply was, "Send him home. I will give him a good beating."

bullying

Bullying is Way Beyond Teasing

Bullying is a part of what happens to far too many children in school. For many adults, we know bullying happens, but we rarely talk about it in a sustained, non-judgmental, age-appropriate manner with children. Sometimes adults see bullying as nothing more than a passage of childhood. However, in this book, you will have an opportunity to see that, for children, being bullied is more than just a simple rite of passage. This book will allow you to have a close-up view of bullying through the experiences of students living in urban and suburban areas of the Greater Milwaukee Community.

Bullying, if ignored, can have a negative and lifelong impact on children as they move from childhood to adulthood; therefore, bullying needs to be addressed as a matter of social justice. Because many cases of in-school bullying occurs repeatedly, any type of bullying, from name calling to threats of physical harm, deprives children of their right to attend school in a safe, just and caring environment.

Everyone Needs to Play a Role to Stop Bullying

All of the following information is from the United States Department of Health and Human Services. For more information on this subject, please go to: www.stopbullyingnow.hrsa.gov.

Schools should be safe environments where any child who is bullied by another student or witnesses bullying behavior knows that such behavior must be reported immediately to an adult.

Some Forms of Bullying

- **Physical Bullying** (hitting, tripping and punching)
- **Verbal Bullying** (name calling such as racial and ethnic slurs)
- **Emotional Bullying** (intimidation using gestures or social exclusion)
- **Cyber Bullying** (sending messages by phone or email)
- **Relational Bullying** (ganging up through banding other students together)

Warning Signs May Be Physical or Emotional

Students who have been bullied often have torn clothing, cuts or bruises, and very few friends. They are often withdrawn and other students may describe them as strange, extremely quiet, or very different from their other peers. Many students who have been bullied are afraid to come to school, do not participate in extra-curricular activities, and isolate themselves from their peers. When approached by an adult, they usually respond in a very shy and insecure manner.

Passive or Reactive Victims

The passive victim turns inward when bullied. He or she may cry or withdraw rather than fight back. The reactive bullying victim is much less common than the passive bullying victim. The reactive victim retaliates when getting bullied and sometimes channels his/her rage and anger into bullying others; especially those who are younger and weaker than himself/herself. In this way, some victims of bullies transform into bullies themselves further perpetuating the abuse. It should also be noted that passive victims, when pushed too far or bullied too much, can unpredictably become extremely aggressive.

What to Do If You Suspect Your Child Is Being Bullied

Parents can be proactive when it comes to bullying by keeping an open line of communication with both their child and their child's teacher. Taking time to actively listen to a child's daily activities offers necessary insight into what is happening during the school day or after school as a child is returning home. Many children fear that parents may make matters worse instead of solving the taunts, jeers, and humiliation brought on by bullies. Patience, understanding, and support are critical. Your child needs to know that you will help him/her to address the problem in a positive manner and that you are glad he/she had the courage to let you know that he/she was being bullied.

Teachers, Staff and Administrators Are Major Role Players In Preventing Bullying

Teaching appropriate and inappropriate responses to bullying is the most effective way to address bullying. When adults see or hear about incidents of bullying, they should immediately take action by reinforcing school rules. Support the bullied children in a way that allows them to regain their self-control, and feel supported and safe from retaliation.

Children Can Be Empowered to Speak Up for Their Friends and Classmates

Empowerment for children who are being bullied or witnessing bullying can happen in a variety of ways which include, but are not limited to, the following:

- Do not bully back.
- If you don't feel comfortable or safe speaking to the child who is bullying, you can say some kind words to the child who is being bullied.
- Tell the child who is being bullied that he/she should tell someone what has happened.
- Pay attention to the other children who see the bullying. If these children are laughing, they too could be a part of the problem.
- Tell an adult what you saw and heard!

Why Don't Some Children Tell When They Are Getting Bullied and What Are the Effects?

Most children may not want others to think they are tattling, afraid, or weak. Some who witness the bullying may be afraid that they may get bullied next. Victims of bullying suffer psychological and sometimes physical scars that last a lifetime. In some cases, victims may turn their anger inward, which may lead to severe depression, anxiety or even suicide.

Building a Safe Community

Bullying is not a normal part of growing up. Therefore, as a learning community, it is critical that students become more conscious of themselves and their conduct.

As a way to build a safe community, the students who participated in this project have reflected, through writings and drawings, their own attitudes, experiences and behaviors toward the sensitive issue of bullying. Through writings, drawings, and reflections, students perceived some things that could bring about positive differences in themselves and others.

Throughout this project, students were provided a platform voice and common vocabulary for discussing how to treat one another fairly in the classroom, on the playground and within their community.

Restorative Justice

PAT LACOCQUE, MILWAUKEE PUBLIC SCHOOL RESTORATIVE JUSTICE FACILITATOR
MARQUETTE UNIVERSITY LAW STUDENTS

"Academic achievement will only flourish in a civil and safe school environment."

Restorative practices address the need for integrating emotional literacy, social skill development, violence prevention and conflict resolution education into the fabric of a school.

Restorative practices are based on Restorative Justice, which has its roots in indigenous practices and values. For example, the Lakota/ Dakota phrase "mitakuye oyasin" which means "we are all related," urges us to create communities of care that support healing in all relationships.

What Is Restorative Justice?

Restorative Justice is a systemic response to wrongdoing that emphasizes healing the wounds of victims, offenders and communities. Restorative principles and practices help:

1. Hold the offender accountable for her/his actions.
2. Provide victims with a safe place to share how the incident impacted her/him.
3. Include members of the community in developing a moral stance and helping the offender in making things right.
4. Develop an effective alternative to the traditional system of punishment.

By "making things right" restorative practices seek to knit wholeness back into a community that has been torn. In schools, restorative practices seek to build relationships so that students can focus on their school work and participate as members of the school's learning community.

Ms. Patricia Lacocque has worked with the Milwaukee Public Schools in implementing "Circles" to build community. Through the power of these community circles, work has been done to reduce and eliminate bullying in participating schools.

Why use Restorative Justice in schools?

- Approach to reduce suspensions
- Actively involve the offender
- Address bullying
- Prevent escalating conflict
- Teach self-motivation and self-discipline
- Encourage accountability and responsibility through personal reflection
- Improve classroom and school climate
- Increase awareness of problems facing children
- Promote collaborative planning
- Create empathy and self-responsibility
- Create and maintain caring communities
- Reduce disconnect students face after suspensions
- Bridge the gap between home and school
- Ensure a sense of belonging for all students
- Teach social skills needed to solve conflicts non-violently
- Help students acquire and practice effective verbal skills

Learning for Life Program

BOY SCOUTS OF AMERICA

A group that is helping to make a difference and provide better choices for young people in our community is the Milwaukee County Council Boy Scouts of America. The following excerpt was taken from a 7th grade honor student's speech that was given to community leaders:

"…the Boy Scouts of America organization has been and always will be an important factor in my life. Last year, I became a Boy Scout… this membership has provided me with the enrichment that I will continue to value forever. I learned about leadership. I learned that it is okay to excel as a student and a young man. I've met and worked with other boys seeking to believe in themselves as well.

The Boy Scouts has also given me both physical and mental strengths. The Boy Scouts organization has welcomed me with open arms and made me feel secure. It is nice to know that no matter where I go in the world, I will find other young men like me, who will take their roles in their communities seriously and who can be counted on to help our cities and nation stay great.

The *Learning for Life* program has helped me strengthen the quality of the character growing and developing inside of me. Character education happens each and every day at my school. All students have discussions and activities about developing yourself into a person of quality. We have talked about: the choices we make and why we made them… what it means to be a good worker and what a good worker looks like…about being responsible and about positive ways to talk to each other without hurting feelings or causing fights…. about gangs and why people join them…and about alternative ways to meet our personal needs for friendship and excitement, without joining bad gangs. Most importantly, we have talked about things as a school that we have never really talked about before.

I just want to say that the Boy Scouts of America organization has not only given me courage and determination to succeed, but it has also made me the honorable young man you see before you. I truly respect the men and women who make this program possible…."

People interested in this program should contact Milwaukee County Council Boy Scouts of America at: http://www.milwaukeeboyscouts.org.

Children's Hospital of Wisconsin
Medical College of Wisconsin

It's all about showing kindness

Each of us needs something from one another. We need, everyday, some kindness from those around us. When someone is getting bullied, we bystanders need to show kindness and help the person hurt by standing up for them or getting help. We need to show kindness to the bully by getting him or her help, too. Our families and teachers want to help us show this kindness to one another. If each of us works to help each other, our schools and neighborhoods will glow and we will live in an amazing world.

Always remember the power of your kindness.

Marlene Melzer-Lange, M.D.
Children's Hospital of Wisconsin

The following websites are related to the Children's Hospital and contain some valuable information about bullying:

www.projectujima.org
www.chw.org
www.BlueKids.org

Stop Bullying

Bullies usually lash out at others because he (or she) is angry about something or hurting from past experiences. For example, many times someone has been abused or maybe they grew up observing those around them using violence as a means of settling differences. We need to understand the different ways that children/teens experience bullying (verbally, mentally and physically), how the bully becomes a bully, how the victim becomes a victim (there can be a fine line between the two), and what can be done to stop bullying as it exists on the continuum of violence.

Earnestine Willis, MD, MPH

Professor

Director, Center for the Advancement of Underserved Children

Children's Hospital of Wisconsin

Medical College of Wisconsin

Brown Bag Chat

BULLYING AT SCHOOL/HOME ACTIVITY

PATRICIA A. ELLIS, ED. D., ASSOCIATE VICE PRESIDENT
OF ENROLLMENT SERVICES CARDINAL STRITCH UNIVERSITY

Die Cube for Brown Bag Chat

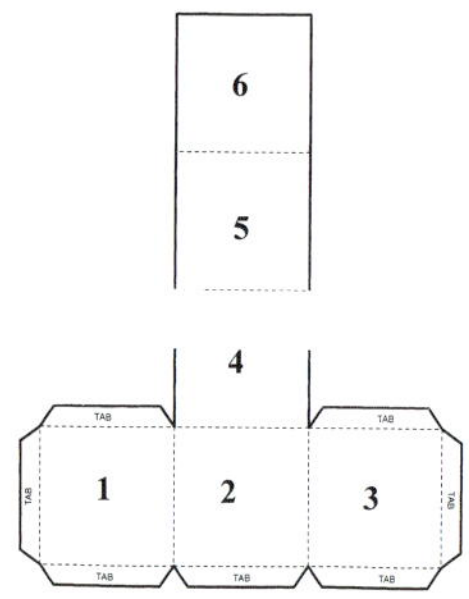

The purpose of this activity for teachers and students or parents/guardians and children is to create an opportunity for you to engage in a casual talk or chat that will enable you to address issues of bullying. A game format is being suggested because oftentimes when students/children are engaged in a game, they are less anxious and more willing to open up and share their heartfelt thoughts and feelings.

Adults are strongly encouraged to engage in this game with your students/children. It is hoped that by playing this game with your students/children, you will be able to begin identifying, discussing, and addressing any possible signs that your students/children may feel bullied or if your students/children may be engaged in bullying types of activities. This game also provides you with an opportunity to share your thoughts, views, and insights on the various questions that are asked during the game.

As you and your students/children play this game, listen for verbal cues, look for physical signs, touch upon key feelings, thoughts or ideas your students/children may share. Ask follow up questions after you have played the game or create and add your own questions to the game in order to gain a better understanding of what your students/children may be feeling as a result of their experiences with bullying.

If you discover that your students/children are being bullied or if they are bullying others, don't ignore the problem. Acknowledge the problem and take action steps to address the bullying immediately. Students/Children need to know that, if they are a victim of bullying, there are caring, supportive adults who will address the problem.

Materials: -Brown lunch bag or shoebox with a lid
-Index cards or strips of paper with questions included in this section
-Die cube

Number of players: 2 or more

Directions: Photocopy and cut into strips or rewrite the questions included in this section on index cards. Place the individual questions in the brown lunch bag or shoebox. You or your students/children may shake the brown lunch bag or covered shoebox of questions. Each player should take a turn rolling the die cube. The player who rolls the highest number should begin the game. Take turns pulling questions from the brown lunch bag or shoebox. As the players take turns pulling and responding to the questions from the brown bag or shoebox, the other players should listen without making any comments to the player's response to the question. If a player pulls a "Special of the Day" card or strip, he/she may create his/her own question about bullying to ask each of the other players.

NOTE: The "Special of the Day" question may be related to the other players' earlier response to a question.

As questions are pulled from the brown lunch bag or shoebox, the player who asks the question should hold onto the question card or strip until the end of the game when all question cards or strips may be placed back into the brown lunch bag or shoebox.

The game is over when all the questions in the brown lunch bag or shoebox have been answered.

Extension Activity: Play the game as often as you like by using the original questions plus questions created by each of the players prior

to the start of the game. Having each of the players create questions to add to the game may provide a wonderful opportunity to have important questions answered or helpful tips and strategies provided in a supportive manner.

Special Note for Playing This Game With Young Children

When playing this game with very young students/children, you may want to read the questions to your students/children and limit the number of questions that are used. Also, instead of not placing the question back in the brown bag or shoebox after it has been answered, you may want to place the question back in the brown bag or shoebox so that your students/children can hear how others would answer the same question. This is a great way for young students/children to learn that there is more than one way to solve a problem or answer a question.

Brown Bag Chat Questions

- In your opinion, what are five things that make a person a bully?
- Why do you think some people become a bully?
- Have you ever been left out of activities? How did you react to being left out?
- If you saw someone being left out of a game or other activity, how do you think that person might feel?
- If you saw someone being treated in a mean or rude manner, what might you do?
- Who is your best friend?
- Name two or more adults you could talk to if you needed help.
- What are things you and your best friend like to do together?
- What are things you and your best friend do not like to do together?
- Have others ever called you hurtful names or teased you? How did it make you feel?
- What do you do when others call you hurtful names or tease you?
- What would you do if others were being called hurtful names or being teased?
- If you were being bullied, what are at least three things you could do?
- If you saw someone else being bullied, what are at least three things you could do?
- Have you ever been afraid to go somewhere because you knew you would be bullied? Explain why.
- How have others made you feel bullied?
- How have you felt when you were being bullied?
- How have you felt when you saw others being bullied?
- Have you ever helped someone who was being bullied? What did you do and what happened as a result of you helping that person?
- In your opinion, what are some things that could be done to stop bullying?
- Would you tell someone if you had been bullied or if you saw someone being bullied? Explain why.
- What are things that you like about yourself? Explain why you like each thing.
- What are things you do to show others you care about them?
- What are two or more things you think you do very well?
- What are two or more things you think you do not do very well?
- "Special of the Day" Card.
- What are two or more things you would like to do someday to help others?
- What could you tell someone who is being bullied to do?
- What could you say to someone who is bullying others?
- If you had to talk to an adult about being bullied, what could you say?
- If you had to talk to an adult about seeing other children being bullied, what could you say?
- What could adults do to help children prevent bullying?
- If someone is made fun of, do you find it funny?
- How do you feel when you see others get their feelings hurt?

Bullying Book Writing Challenge

PATRICIA A. ELLIS, ED. D., ASSOCIATE VICE PRESIDENT OF ENROLLMENT SERVICES
SCOTT RUDIE , ASSISTANT DIRECTOR, PUBLIC RELATIONS
CARDINAL STRITCH UNIVERSITY

Putting pencil or pen to paper can have a very positive effect when children witness or experience bullying. By writing, children have opportunities to express feelings, emotions, and thoughts that are sometimes difficult to express through spoken words. The writing challenge topics below are being provided as a way to give students/children an opportunity to freely express their views on bullying. For some, this may mean a collage of words and pictures while for others it may mean writing and illustrating a short story. The form that your students'/children's writing takes should be left to their discretion because the primary purpose of this writing challenge is for your students/children to have an opportunity to express their feelings, emotions, and thoughts about a topic that far too many have personally observed or experienced.

Your students/children may create their own writing challenge topic, or they may choose any of the topics listed below for their writing challenge:

What I Can Do to Create a No Bullying Zone at School

Write about things that you can do to make your school a safe and welcoming place for all students.

How to Avoid Falling Into the Bullying Trap

Write about why you think bullies become bullies and how you think they can stop being bullies.

The Importance of Standing Strong and Being True to Yourself

Create an advice column about how people can avoid becoming the victims of bullies and/or becoming bullies.

Who Can I Turn To?

Write a friendly letter to someone you know who has been a victim of bullying with suggestions for who they can talk to about their problem and feelings.

Helpful Tips for Educators and Parents/Guardians

Encourage your students/children to include some of the vocabulary words (located in the glossary) from this book in their short story, poem, letter, rap, word collage, etc. as a way to further develop their written and oral communications skills.

Suggested Writing Process

1. **Prewriting:** Students/Children should take the time to reflect upon or think about what they are going to write about bullying including how it has affected them and how they have reacted to bullying.
2. **Writing:** Students'/Children's voices should be reflected in their writing. In other words, encourage your students/children to write from their heart. Teachers/Parents should encourage students/children to be open and honest as they write. Share with your students/children that their work will be considered confidential unless it includes information that may involve their personal well being or the well being of someone else. In either case, let them know that their concerns are being heard and will be addressed.
3. **Revise/Edit/Publish:** Students/Children should be encouraged to develop and revise their writing to a publishable copy. This will give them greater ownership of their writing, allow their authentic voice to come through in their writing, and promote proofreading and editing to produce a publishable piece.

Bullying Connections Self Guided Tour of the Milwaukee Art Museum

BARBARA BROWN-LEE, CHIEF EDUCATOR, MILWAUKEE ART MUSEUM

The following pieces were selected to demonstrate artists' interpretation of violence and aggression. These works attempt to depict cultural impacts, visual interest, and universal languages that express emotion. We welcome you to a "self tour" of the Milwaukee Art Museum's collections.

1. Mary T. Smith "Two People" M1997.13 (Ross-Pain Gallery; Folk Art Collection)

Mary Smith worked with limited color and broad strokes that focused on voodooish faces reminiscent of African masks. Her paintings reflect her life as a simple yet complex individual who found herself independent and painted with a style all her own. The struggles of her youth and working as a servant provided her much solitude and strife. However, she was able to create spaces in spaces and work swiftly demonstrating conflict or reflection of the world around her.

2. Riguad Benoit (1966) "Fighting With Stick" M199.112 (Haitian Art Collection)

Haitian Artist who worked very slowly on this piece of art, and it reveals the complexity of the religion and the intersection of Haiti's African origins with Christian beliefs. Self taught artist who recognized the importance of capturing the artistic output of a nation, which despite ongoing political turmoil, maintained the importance of Haitian art and culture.

3. Unknown "Pair of Black Figures" M1989 126a.b. (Ross-Pain Gallery; Folk Art Collection)

A "Pair of Black Figures" is attributed to a black artist because they are not done in a caricature of African-Americans at the time. They are formed as a part of a larger ceremonial ensemble. Their origin is unknown, yet Maltese cross suggest ties to Free Masons or black fraternal organizations which were quite prevalent in the late 19th century in southern Ohio (an antique dealer bought them off a front porch sale). They were possibly used in funeral rites and were made to be seen in the round. One figure holds a possible ceremonial staff in his clenched fist, and the other holds a bible or book. Their faces represent African masks in their simplest form. This tranquil expression is a sign of nobility in African sculpture.

4. Edgar Tolson "Cain Slaying Abel" M1989.315.6 (Ross-Pain Gallery; Folk Art Collection)

In this scene of the Fall of Man series, Tolson demonstrates the moment just before Cain kills Abel. Abel sees the stick and knows what his brother is about to do to him for he is cognizant that he is going to die. Cain makes a decision that will determine his lot in life as well as that of all humankind. Tolson shows Cain with a toga over his right shoulder and Abel over his left.

5. Rosemarie Koczy "Weaving Tapestry" M1994.126, M1994.102, M1994.95 (Ross-Pain Gallery)

Skeletal figures barely emerging from their densely hatched backgrounds, appearing almost too weak to break on the surface. Koczy's drawings are something she cannot control for she does them with both hands simultaneously. She spent time in the concentration camps during World War II and still is haunted by the memories today.

6. Rufino Tamayo M1963.145A (Bradley Collection)

Mexican artist, Tamayo, was influenced by his interest in the heritage of the Mexican Indians and their Pre-Columbian ancestors. He was nurtured by Picasso's geometric art especially

the Cubism. His art demonstrates a blend of both the 20th century artistic revolution and of primitive collections.

7. Wassily Kandinsky Abstract M1958.12 (Bradley Collection)

The artist attempted to create a universal language that expressed abstract emotions.

"Color is the keyboard, the eyes are the hammer, and the soul is the piano with many strings." Kandinsky created simple representations of objects into a spiritual realm where color and rhythm act as the communicating agents which inspire the inner self. Concentric circles which indicate an explosion and black crosshatchings represented barbed-wire fences express an awareness of the war talk surrounding him at the time he painted this in 1913.

8. Fernand Leger "The Wounded II" M1977.118 (Bradley Collection)

His geometric forms in contrasting colors had become more abstractly simplified. It is still possible to see a bandaged head with a closed eye and an arm composed of fragmented cylinders. This image is perhaps associated with Leger's injuries incurred during World War I. His work is influenced by Cubism and his personal view of man in the modern world.

9. Picasso "Cock of Liberation" M1959.372 (Bradley Collection)

Picasso's increased interest in political events developed during the 1930's. He was deeply affected by the events of the departure of the Nazi troops from occupied Paris in the fall of 1944, the crucial step of the liberation of France. This exuberant color gives expression and energetic brushwork of all of France upon their release from tyranny. The Gallic Cock was recognized as a symbol of the French people, and it has once again regained its vibrant splendor. Picasso showed this as a cry of victory and optimism. The artist had used images of animals and these particular animals demonstrate pride and often ferocious tenacity. It allows one to look ahead to brighter days of hope and endurance.

10. Marino Marini "Battle" M1963.140 (Bradley Collection)

Marini traveled extensively attempting to become immersed in different cultures as he experimented with conflict and its different forms. Like his ancestors, he chose horses as a symbol for struggle and strife. His interest in this theme evolved from the Etruscans, for whom the horse was a symbol of man revolting against the static laws of fate.

11. Marino Marini "Sculpture" M1977.122 (Bradley Collection)

Ancient idea is saturated with a modern tone. With terrible fury, the horse strains its head and neck upward in a spiritual and physical defiance of both fate and gravity. A single mass of muscle and tendon are detailed and simplified to resemble a projectile. The sharp edges, shining planes, and rough spaces charge the bronze with reality and tension.

12. Kehinde Wiley "St. Dionysus" M2006.16 (Gallery #28)

Kehinde Wiley, created lifelike—and life-sized—portraits of break-dancing boys in classical poses. Wiley presents his young men as heroic, pathetic, autonomous and manipulated. Ultimately, Wiley's practice disturbs and interrupts the commonality of portrait painting. His goal is to locate "class struggle at the level of sign." Wiley often takes poor models and makes them into a sense of icons depending on the attire and structure. His portraits are based on photographs of young men who Wiley sees on the street, begun last year with men mostly from Harlem's 125th Street. The series now includes models from the South Central neighborhood where he was born.

13. Schabel "Broken Plates" M1986.76 (Gallery #26)

His works exhibit an ambivalent emotional tone, jarring color harmonies, and a primitive style of multi-layered imagery. This work refers to a friend living in a communist part of a country. The broken plates themselves convey the archaeological layers of the Eternal City. The fragments of history and everyday life including the destructive (smashing) and reconstructive (painting) process of creation itself, and the fluid mixture of all these elements in the artist's consciousness—all in a work of overwhelming power.

14. Anselon Kiefer M1987.1 (Gallery #27)

The fragility of his work is contrasted against the stark subject matter in his paintings. The theme of all the work is the trauma experienced by entire societies, and the continual rebirth and renewal in life. Drawing from his past, many controversial works are sought to convey a sense of history especially from the Nazi influence in Germany. The burned and scarred settings include a possible reference to the Roman occupation of Germany. This strong sense of destruction and regeneration of Germany's historic consciousness and recent past are believed to be present.

15. Georg Baselitz M1989.1 (Gallery #27)

Georg Baselitz's monumental, somber work was painted during a decade of well-being in Germany, when the generation of the wirtschaftswunder—the economic miracle—was only interrupted in its relentless quest for stable prosperity by the occasional political scandal or terrorist attack.

16. Sigmar Polke M1987.5 (Gallery #27)

The powerful statement of bars withholding a something inside that is obscure. The lurid and magisterial renderings of prison bars and camps remind us of past abominations such as checkpoints, war, fires, and souls, in a world inflamed by power and countries surrounded by threats.

17. Alfred Leslie, 1970 "Alfred Leslie" L1970.13 (Gallery #20)

His intent is to magnify the fact that the viewer is being confronted by another human being. In this portrait of the artist, he is clad in Roman tunic, hammer in one hand, the other is clenched and wounded, the face contorted in an anguished grimace. Filling the viewer's field of vision with this rigid, frontal figure, the artist has painted not only himself but about himself in a way that demands reaction.

18. Roy Lichtenstein "Crying Girl" M1965.18 (Gallery #19)

The artist has effectively controlled the emotions by using a comic strip format to dehumanize the subject. Although dehumanized, we still feel the pain and anguish and taste the tears of her sadness. Lichtenstein made this into a "style of industrialization" and plays into a clairvoyant awareness of the 20th century trials and tribulations. This emulated America in the 1960's as he looked to radically challenge modern art such as society brought many challenges.

19. Alexander Archipenko "Boxers" M1983.189 (Gallery #16)

This organizes two pugilists (fighters using fists) in a composition of interlocking action and counteraction. The negative spaces between the two struggling figures and their dynamic counterpoint express confrontation forms. As seen as a sport of sparring with fists, there assumes a great amount of respect for each figure. From different views, one can see surprising distinct aspects and profiles.

20. Stuart Davis, "Tenement Scene" 1912 M1973.607 (Gallery #15)

The urban setting displays a rather dark environment including loneliness and solitude. The artist uses a tone that exemplifies an urban setting with a worrisome look with darkness and grayscales.

Glossary

Abuse: to attack in words or physically

Aggression: an attack made without reasonable cause

Anger: a strong feeling of displeasure and usually of opposition toward someone or something

Anxiety: fear or nervousness about what might happen

Bitterness: causing sharp physical or mental pain or discomfort

Bully: a person who teases, hurts, or threatens smaller or weaker persons

Bystander: a person standing near but taking no part in what is happening

Coerce: to force to act or think in a given way by pressure, threats, or intimidation

Confront: to face, especially in challenge

Cruel: causing or helping to cause suffering

Discuss: to consider carefully and openly by reasoning or argument

Emotion: a mental reaction (as anger or fear) marked by strong feeling and usually causing physical effects

Explode: to burst or cause to burst with violence and noise

Fear: an unpleasant often strong emotion caused by expectation or awareness of danger

Guilt: the state of one who has done something wrong

Harass: to create an unpleasant situation for someone by unwelcome verbal or physical conduct

Health: the condition of being sound in body, mind, or spirit; especially: freedom from disease

Humiliate: cause to lose pride or self-respect

Imperfection: the quality or state of being flawed

Intervene: to come between in order to stop, settle, or change

Intimidate: to make timid or fearful by or as if by threats

Irate: threatening as if in anger

Loneliness: to be without another being or by oneself

Panic: a sudden overpowering fright, especially without reasonable cause

Physical: of or relating to the body

Prevent: to keep from happening

Protect: to cover or shield from something that would destroy or injure

Retaliate: to return like for like, especially to return evil for evil

Restorative justice: to put back the quality of being fair or just to a situation

Role model: a person whose behavior in a certain role is imitated by others

Scared: feeling alarm or fright

Secure: providing safety

Senses: a specialized function or mechanism (as sight, hearing, smell, taste, or touch) of the body that involves the action and effect of a stimulus on a sense organ

Solution: an answer to a problem

Tease: to annoy continually or make fun of another

Tolerance: sympathy for or acceptance of feelings, habits, or beliefs that are different from one's own

Victim: a person cheated, fooled, or harmed by another

Reflect: to think seriously and carefully

Source: the Merriam-Webster Online Dictionary

Resources

Amstutz & Mullet, The Little Book of Restorative Discipline for Schools, (Intercourse, PA: Good Books, 2005).

Burstyn, Joan N. "Involving the Whole School in Violence Prevention," Preventing Violence in Schools: A Challenge to American Democracy, (2001).

Morrison, Brenda, "Bullying and Victimization in Schools: A Restorative Justice Approach," Trends in Issues in Crime and Criminal Justice, Feb. 2002.

www.stopbullyingnow.hrsa.gov. United States Department of Health and Human Services

Bibliography

Goldstein, Rosalie, ed. Guide to the Collections. Milwaukee: Burton & Meyer, 1986.

Neff, Teri Ann, ed. Building a Masterpiece. New York: Hudson Hills Press, 2001.

SHARP Literacy, Inc.

SHARP (Student Historical Art Resource Program) creates a learning environment for elementary school students to enhance lessons and build core competencies in history, science and language through visual arts and art history. SHARP's programs encourage students to research, read, write and then present their creative work. SHARP Literacy, Inc. is a nonprofit 501(c)(3) education program based in Milwaukee, Wisconsin.

Formal assessment of the SHARP Literacy program by Applied Measurement and Evaluation Services has shown the following:

- The mission of integrating the visual arts and art history into the science, language arts and social studies curriculum has content validity.
- Students in the SHARP Literacy program have dramatically increased vocabulary skills compared to those who are not a part of the program.
- Students have increased writing skills and comprehension of material learned.
- The SHARP program is an effective tool in decreasing discipline problems for many at-risk students.

SHARP Literacy expands horizons and bolsters reading and writing abilities. The program also represents a dynamic, interactive response to the philosophical concept of "no children left behind" in our school systems.

For more information about SHARP Literacy, Inc., visit www.creativesharp.org or call 414-270-3388.